Poetry Diversified 2018

A Human Experience Anthology

Compiled by Lucinda J. Clark

Copyright © 2018 P.R.A. Publishing

All rights reserved. Except for brief passages quoted in a newspaper, magazine, radio, television or blog review, no part of this book may be reproduced in any form or by any means, electronic or mechanical, including photocopying and recording or by any information storage and retrieval system without permission in writing from the Publisher. Copyright ownership for each poem remains with the poet whose name appears with the title.

ISBN: 978-1941416-25-9 (paperback)
ISBN: 978-1941416-16-7 (eBook)
ISBN: 978-1941416-17-4 (Mobi)
Library of Congress Catalog Number: 2018938055

P.R.A. Publishing
P.O. Box 211701
Martinez, GA 30917
www.prapublishing.com

Cover design by Rada Kuznetsova.
Interior design by Medlar Publishing Solutions Pvt Ltd., India.

Printed in the United States.

For Spring Robinson
aka
Mahogany Red

May 7, 1987 - January 16, 2016

Acknowledgments

This edition of Poetry Diversified comes as we celebrate our eighteenth year of awarding literary prizes for emerging voices. We have so many people to thank for our continued success. First, there are the volunteers that judge. To my children; Jeska and Xavier Clark who have been judging since its beginning. They are now in their mid-twenties and keep their schedules open when the call to judge comes even now. To Pauline Findlay, Sharon Schroeder, Calvin Pennywell and Leah Smith.

To Tulane University remote interns Rada Kuznetsova for her thoughtful introduction and painstaking effort to stay true to poet's intentions while editing. Kayla Davis who worked on review with intent to learn as much about the process of putting an anthology together.

To the teachers who encourage students to enter year after year like Jen Karetnick of Miami Arts Charter Schools. It has been a pleasure reading the thoughts of the future minds you shape.

To Laura Macdonald, our newest team member, who came to the party late but asked the one question that kept this project and several others on track. While I could go on I will stop here because you, dear reader, want to get on with it. Enjoy.

Table of Contents

Introduction . . . . *ix*

2016 Winners

Middle School Category 3
Suspenseful City (Mateo Strickland). 4
Downcast (Isabella Matthei) 5
Regrets (Alana Olivero) 6
Fake (Maia Tasker) 7

High School Category 9
The Number Game (Daniela Antelo) 10
Dear Abuela (Naomi Jeanpierre). 12
Cosmic Soul (Nyaila Newbold) .13
The Mask (Allyson Ifergan). 14

Adult Category 15
You Became My Father (Gina Marie Mammano). 16
Hairology (Amanda O'Mara). 18
That Brilliant Samba (David Morgan O'Connor). 20
Lighthouse (Melanie Lucht) 21

Senior Category 23
Never at Rest (Nancy Louise Cook) 24
Barefoot in Montgomery (Lee Patton) 26
Jack's Commitments (Robert Ronnow) 28

Table of Contents

International Poet Category 31
Mapendo (Mima Kabwe) 32
I Procrastinated (Graca N. Kibio). 34
Hope (Siya Ntsumpa) 35
The Wayfarer's Waterloo (Yvonne Wedgwood) 36

2017 Winners

Middle School Dave Drake Award 41
To the Willow (Elyse Thomas) 42
The Anatomy of Hope (Angelina Minnittee) 44
Trumpet of the Herald (Turner Toliuszis) 45
Why Choose to Risk It (Lily Barmoha) 46

High School Category – Aiken 47
Supernatural (Cameron Barron) 48
Fragile (Jasmine Kitchings) 49
Colors (Lizzy Kleinkauf) 50
Building Block (Brandi De Haven). 51

High School Category – International 53
If Forgiveness Was Made of Stardust
    (Sophia Giudici-Juarez). 54
The Infinity of Possibility (Marina Ellis). 56
Her Voice (Jennifer Nguyen) 57
Death of the Poèt (Nadia Dimtrova). 59

Adult Mahogany Red Literary Prize. 61
Racist Rice (Minncey Richani) 62
Diamonds on the Rocks (Ellen Ricks) 64

Table of Contents

The Death of a Poet (Kendall Driscoll) 66
Paradise in Tears (Masoyo Has) .68
Impatience (Noel Pratt) 70

Senior Category 71
Red Ink on Miracles (Wendy MacLean) 72
The Last Wildflower (Don Shook) 73
Fear of Fire. Lower East Side, 1966 (Terence Cady) 74
Ode to the Ravioli I Left Behind (Dianalee Velie) 76

Winner Biographies 77

Introduction

My name is Rada Kuznetsova and I am an intern at Poetry Matters Project. Currently, I am an undergraduate student at Tulane University in New Orleans, LA majoring in English and Art History. Coincidentally, I am also one of the few lucky people who got a chance to work with Poetry Diversified anthology series. The Poetry Matters Project and this book are my debuts in the publishing industry. I hope to become a book editor after I graduate and this became a great starting point for me. I was looking for an internship opportunity through the TRIP program at Tulane University, so I could gain some experience in the literary world. Then, I stumbled upon the Poetry Matters Project. I have never really done editing in the past, so I was entirely unprepared for how much I would love it.

I feel tremendously lucky to even be a small part of this anthology. As I was reading the poems, I could not help but be amazed at the variety and talent seen in these works. All the poets come from a wide range of countries and age groups. Collections with such diversity can be quite rare. The Middle School section was especially surprising. Those poems are philosophical and introspective in nature, addressing social and cultural issues that many adults don't even think about. Once again, these students teach us not to dismiss anyone based on their age.

Introduction

A few poems in particular caught my attention. "The Number Game" by Daniela Antelo was well-structured and unique in its approach. The poet's decision to mix words and numbers was especially interesting. My absolute favourite was an "An Ode to the Ravioli I Left Behind" by Dianalee Velie. The poem can be seen as a clever reminder to the readers that it is the small things in life than often matter most, but personally, I loved it for its humour. I believe it's important to recall, from time to time, that poetry can be funny, meaningful and beautiful, all at the same time.

In the end, Poetry Diversified 2018 and Poetry Matters Project helped me to become even more passionate not just about the idea of editing but the job itself. It became an experience I could hardly hope for and will always treasure.

2016 Winners

Middle School Category
High School Category
Adult Category
Senior Category
International Poet Category

Middle School Category

Suspenseful City

Mateo Strickland

Skyscrapers tower over the magazine kiosks.
Middle aged men in fancy suits,
Handing out checks and dollar bills,
like the pieces of paper they really are.
Patches of trees and grass,
surrounded by sewage-scented concrete.
This is where a washer and a dryer in your own apartment,
Means you've made it.
Warm water and air conditioning are luxuries.
And a car is a precious possession,
until you are emerged in the line of immobile cars.
This is where an average citizen
has more stories of adventure, surprise and excitement,
than any other American could dream of.
Where everywhere you go,
you never know what'll happen.

Downcast

Isabella Matthei

I don't have the ability to go back in time,
but I saw what I saw.
The sorrowful faces of all my classmates
seems like a memory already relieved.

The footsteps as loud as metal dropping on a concrete floor.
The thoughts of people ever popping out.
But that's the day I lost the people I loved.

The screams haunt me when I go to sleep,
and the aftermath will never leave my head.
But I like to assume that things will all be okay.

The circle of life is there for a reason,
because we all go through it.
You only live once, so don't make it a negative place.

Regrets

Alana Olivero

We choose to kill someone,
yet we are afraid to die.
Does it mean nothing,
to see that person's loved one start to cry?

When you meet death in the eye,

Do all your regrets and pain hurt
because you finally realize,
This is how you made your life to be?

FAKE

Maia Tasker

From the moment I wake up,
to the moment I lie down in bed,
I wear a mask.
A joyful face-smiling,
mechanical laughter,
computer-generated sentences.
Behind it I sit,
screaming and sobbing.
Trapped in a nightmare
some call life.
Banging against the
plastic edges of this
mannequin body.
I want to be free-
rid myself of the
mask, tear away this
lifeless, plastic body.

High School Category

The Number Game

Daniela Antelo

130.
The confidence she craved was
buried in the marrow of her bones.
Self-loathing became the dictator
of her thoughts; she was at war.

115.
Hatred knows no boundaries.
Meals were scarce,
exercise was mandatory,
no battles could be lost.

100.
Obsession ran thick through her veins,
creating the perfect soldier.
The shadow of disease made its home
in the jagged outlines of her face.

85.
Her weak pulse and light breaths
were the only proof that the skeleton
of the woman was still alive.

The Number Game

She was housing the enemy
of her own war, feeding it with every
meal she skipped and pound she lost.

The battles continued. If only she knew
confidence cannot be found in bones,
or numbers, but instead in the minds of those
wise enough to love what they don't like.

Dear Abuela

Naomi Jeanpierre

Dear Grandma,
You're a Rubik's cube.
I toss and turn you from one palm to the next,
looking at different angles,
yet no matter how much you twist and turn
I am as perplexed as before.

How many times have we sat at opposite ends,
staring silently,
too afraid to even try to let
our languages muddle together?

Your eyes shine with intelligence.
Like an obscure poem full of flowery prose,
I wonder what your words mean,
but my limited vocabulary fails me.

I'm sorry for being so mute,
for not even trying to scale the wall separating us,
just staring at the obstacle
with awe and fear.

Sincerely, Naomi

Cosmic Soul

Nyaila Newbold

She has a cosmic soul.
Bold black lines run from her head to her toe
and envelope her exterior.
Dull words roll off a vibrant tongue.
Robotic statements formulate in a brain
capable of manifesting planets and galaxies
so massive that the universe is forced to expand.
But this world expects nothing but normality.
She is locked behind skin and bone and teeth
in the cage that is her body.

The Mask

Allyson Ifergan

I'm no different from a puzzle with missing pieces
Trying to find myself as I pick up the lost fragmented bits
Still working on myself, but I know plenty already.
I am incomplete.
I am made of paper.
I am colored in with pencils.
I am just a disguise
still incomplete yet
still magic
still a fire, crumbling.

Every word you throw at me,
turns to ashes before your very eyes.
Lay your tiniest finger on me,
You'll get the worst burn of your life.
I am a force to be reckoned with.

Everything I touch becomes golden.
Potential rushes from my mind to my fingertips.
The impossible can be possible if I believe,
I am magic.
I am made of this, yet to you
I am just this small mask.

Adult Category

You Became My Father

Gina Marie Mammano

You became my father
at the side of the road,

holding up the horizon on highway 190,
you, not me, sticky fingers delivering parenthood
into existence among the ice
–
cold chicken picnic,
a basket reception packed by
mom, slices of celebratory
thick chocolate cake among the succulents.
It was Death Valley. You had no idea that
hot air and salt flats would be the place of your making,
birth among death, Devil's Hole, Badwater Basin,
Furnace Creek, entering life among
the surprise flutter
of flowers, impossible spring bouquets, decorating
the desert floor of your delivery.
We stopped. No, you stopped, in the middle of somewhere.
Slammed chunk
metal doors of the Ford Galaxy and
decided to live out the sugar of the moment,
sit in the arms of mother sun, and be a newborn to the day,
a parent to the offspring of spontaneity.

You Became My Father

I gazed up in wonder,
meeting you for the first time.
The sand got in our eyes, salted our throats,
in the midst of silent spirits of desert fathers,
abbas, ammas smoking their golden incense balls into
wisps of horsetail clouds, marking the wind,
the wild verbena, setting the sand and sky
with the baptism of your selfhood.

HAIROLOGY

Amanda O'Mara

"HAIROLOGY," for Growth and Development:
Understanding Our Roots

Exaggerating this follicle with sweet warmth
and classical lights,
holding tight to one's end, producing while protruding

Easily swaying into clean air;
it has no particular message to send.
Is somewhat content,
settling into a month's new ways until the next,
when all the hype is all the rage.

With confidence, is out like a blaze and fiery spontaneity,
craving adventure and nothing less.

Stuffed with nourishment, those are blessed
if so lucky caress.
What once is singular has found ground with so many alike.
Now it is a local.
To attempt uniqueness becomes obsolete
until the next come to town.
Until then, it is running around,
asserting the right to be vocal.

Hairology

It has finally become full and the head is plump.
If it could verbalize endeavors;
it would do so via the oily and clumsy sounds of a trombone.
Now... what to do about those in a rapid stage
(of growth upon my rump)?

That Brilliant Samba

David Morgan O'Connor

On Rua Mercado
in the center of Rio de Janeiro
there is a samba
that will break your heart
with future sadness
you haven't even imagined yet.
Even if you believe you don't have a heart anymore.
Stronger than a child's death
a brother's cancer
Love's final kiss—depression,
sadder than suicide
lingers only seconds
longer lasting than most marriages...
but there is a secret which is even sadder
you can only hear that brilliant samba
if you are truly alone
with nowhere to go
and nothing to do
at complete loose ends
taking a rest
between bars.

Lighthouse

Melanie Lucht

it's just a pillar between the waves
touching something out of the way
bringing light between two lives
before the sun comes up one more time

erase the past, leave it all in the dark
give everything a new start
take away the endless night
put in the sky, a shining light

two pirates from a missing ship
lying on different sides of the same ocean
waves and storms between them
and so much left unspoken

not even the slightest spark
could empty the darkness between them

but a lighthouse in between
made two pirates cross the sea
for something they both loved to see

Lighthouse

a lighthouse is just a pillar between the waves
touching something out of the way
bringing light between two lives
before the sun comes up one more time

an ocean of storms is one that's tough to cross
but the lighthouse shines a light
through the rain in the dark

across the storms and wreckage
two pirates commit to something they can agree on loving

a lighthouse shines a light between the waves
touching something out of the way
the light that brings two pirates together
while the sun comes up one last time

Senior Category

Never at Rest

Nancy Louise Cook

Here rests a boy
    loved by a mother,

loved by a woman,
    loved by his friends.

He was a boy
    learning to walk at age one.

He was a boy
    learning to pray at age two.

When last seen on a day
    of thanksgiving, he said

he had faith,
    he honored his God, but

he spoke in sorrow
    of how men had failed

God, had seized and
    abused the power of love.

The boy spoke
    of the Father, he spoke of

Never at Rest

Brother Malcolm,
    of souls and the spirit lost.

He was speaking of
    radical Islam. He was speaking

of the United States. Here rests that child.

He was a boy
    killed by a boy.

He was a boy
    killing a boy.

And there is no rest
    for the mothers.

Barefoot in Montgomery

Lee Patton

My best black loafers bore me to so many weddings,
school socials, and funerals
I thought they were good for this trip,
but they thought not and began to protest near the Southern
Poverty Law Center just as scores of school kids convened
around Maya Lin's fountain memorial to civil rights
demonstrators, kids listless until their teacher told them they
could dunk their fingers in the water.

The ruckus gave me cover as I side-stepped the slippery
backsplash, my shoe sole wobbling under me, which,
unglued, had dragged me through
The White House of the Confederacy
and now, back to Dexter Avenue
where I would not have been able to flee
the attackers' baseball bat bludgeons
had I been a Freedom Rider in '61, pulverized for want
of a steady sole,
hobbled in place right where the march
ended in '65, arrived on foot from Selma where thousands
gathered under the Capitol. There on the corner of Dexter
and Decatur my soles finally flipped off
and I could not proceed

Barefoot in Montgomery

until I chucked the loafers in the trash
and climbed the Capitol steps
to overlook the bland, bleached city
barefoot as an old-time penitent
stymied in the distance between
the laced-up emptiness of Montgomery
and the slow-stepping ache of history.

Jack's Commitments

Robert Ronnow

These are Jack's commitments: to his body
exercise, stretch, heal if possible and prepare for death.
To his sons: love and respect and teach, learn
to be aware of the effects of his anger or forever
be an angry man.

To his wife: in equal portions serenity and uncertainty,
the early years, the middle years, and the final years.
To the community: to treat it as distinct unknowable
individuals
much like heavenly spirits but also dangerous animals.

To poetry, religious in its contemplation
of experience under the eye of eternity,
in the realm of the gift and the realm of the sacred:
his individual experiment gone well or wrong.

To his student: not to hurt for gain or inflict more pain
than stimulates growth. Both are students
of each other, the periodic table and the civil war.
Other than that, expect to forget and be forgotten.

Jack's Commitments

To his friends who are merely friendly: lonely
inexorably, working hard and playing hard without self-pity
severe about the law and believing in the death penalty
they're the men you'll want in your foxhole warriors at
the gate.

To himself by which I mean mind or something hidden,
intestate:
a quiet place and time to think deeply or simply
but not too easily to quiet the questions, to know
his bones and the particles of sunlight they stilled
and slowed.

International Poet Category

MAPENDO

Mima Kabwe

Mapendo…..
Her name means love.
It is beautifully pronounced,
and announced
in Swahili tongue,
but Mapendo is a direct contradiction
to the admiration
of her name.
She has self-hate tattooed in ghostly tears,
Destruction enveloped in suicidal chants,
and emotions bottled in hypocritical smiles.

Her Mother calls her Mama,
And "Nukupenda" (I love you), is uttered to
her each morning.
Followed by the tales of how, the magic in her ethnic
features exhibits beauty undefined,
Beauty preconceived,
That can never be confined.
Her mother explains that, the swarthy pigment of
her skin boasts,
of being kissed by the sun,
and her flaws make her human.
and that her thick cotton hair is her crown,

Mapendo

but depositions
of previous invasions
of self-hate surround her pupils.
Drenched in insecurities
insinuated by the Media's lies.

Her cries
are of silent melodies.
She searches for clarity

in preconceived norms of beauty.
With the depiction
Of her reflection,
being nothing but imperfection,
BEAUTY becomes her addiction.
So she seeks solace in bleached skin.
Acceptance in extensions.
Joy in illusions,
And hope in confusion.
She is oblivious to the fact that she is
Mapendo,
and Mapendo is everything that is beautiful.

I Procrastinated

Graca N. Kibio

Dear Future Children,
Do not procrastinate.
Eat your vegetables (except for brussels sprouts).
Do not let anyone tell you not to wear orange because
it makes you look fat. Fat is a concept not
a reality.
Love your friends. Love your enemies. Love yourself.
Fall in love but don't lose yourself in the process.
Read Maya Angelou. I suggest "I Know Why the Caged
Bird Sings."
Do not procrastinate.
Find God.
Never utter the word "YOLO" in my house. This may be
the only thing I'll disown you for.
Give back to the community that raised you.
Listen to 2pac.
Be bold, be loving, be kind, be you.
And please,
do not procrastinate.

HOPE

Siya Ntsumpa

We watch, waiting wearily, while waves wash to shore
traces of our belongings on this island we fear to explore.
The journey disrupted by an
unforeseen and disastrous storm,
completely capsizing the commodious 'Crusader' to never
return to form.
By now those awaiting our arrival must have deduced
something's amiss.
Sparking questions,
consulting experts who'll reach a conclusion close to this.
There are surely ships scheduled to
sail soon in search of stranded survivors,
hope allows us to believe!
Hope, therefore, shields
us.
It yields despondency and its by-product desperation
from ushering our souls into an abyss
we'll be unable to retrieve.

The Wayfarer's Waterloo

Yvonne Wedgwood

Strands of sea grass dancing, caressed by ocean swell
Rusty hull and anchor – now silent the ship's bell.
Shell-encrusted yellow sand – a blanket for your bones
Welcome to the locker – of your host – Davey Jones.

Now your final resting place for all eternity
Beloved kith and kin on shore never more to see
No more to feel the sunlight, nor smell the salty breeze
Nor feel the lift of a heaving deck, buckling 'neath your knees.

Your luck's run out, you must accept, the direst of all fates
No more ashore in foreign ports carousing with your mates
In squalid bars, where poxy tarts relieve your hot desire
No more ale or fiery rum to set your soul on fire.

No more there'll be sea shanties flowing from your lips
No more brawls with shipmates, or crews from rival ships
Over whores, a cheating card game, or ancient debt unpaid.
No more a girl in every port – no more to be betrayed.

Down here no one gives a damn about your earthly past
Whether you were novice or spent years before the mast
Or whether you made captain or stayed part of the crew
Down here all souls are equal – Lascar, Brit or Jew.

The Wayfarer's Waterloo

Though dashing you may once have been, handsome
I've no doubt
Your face is now a grinning skull – but what's to smile about?
For you are doomed to lie here 'till the briny eats your bones
Forever in the arms – of your keeper – Davey Jones.

2017 Winners

Middle School Dave Drake Award
High School Category – Aiken
High School Category – International
Adult Mahogany Red Literary Prize
Senior Category

Middle School Dave Drake Award

To the Willow

Elyse Thomas

I used to think you were my mother.
Your branches would cradle me in a tight bundle
of gnarled wood, letting my arms slip out at the top,
so I could break off the splintered blemishes
along your fingertips. At nights, I'd finger the braided edges
of your curtained, green hair as you caressed
my caramel cheeks to sleep.
Sometimes, I'd believe you were my jungle gym,
my bare feet kissing your outstretched arms
while my hands searched for folds in your skin,
letting me climb to the top and wrap my legs
around the rim of your neck. Then,
I'd grab your nearest braid and balance my weight
on your lifeless hair, swinging to the ground.
When the heavy burdens of life
would weigh upon my frail shoulders,
I'd dig into the earthy flesh surrounding your legs
and cake my fingernails with the dried soil by your stump.
My heart would race, and I'd scream the hurtful words
of gardening tools, threatening to damage your bark
and scrape off the dried remains of your flesh.

To the Willow

But I am old and weary now,
and I have been told you are not for me anymore.
I cannot love you, or play with you, or hate you;
I can just watch you lay in a deafening silence,
your fingertips stiff and your hair limp,
unlike how you used to be.

The Anatomy of Hope

Angelina Minnittee

Hope is such a fragile thing,
like a home made out of playing cards. It is too easy to tumble over.
Hope is as tough as a rock at the same time, protecting its dream
like a soldier does his country.
Hope is a brick wall of faith inside that can still fracture like bones and collapse at any moment.
For me, hope is the ringing of bells on a door, welcoming wanderers that are treated just like family but my heart wakes up as empty as always.
A man walks through a street,
asking for that tiny piece of paper
that seems to make this world go round,
while all who surround him
brush him off
as if he were a ghost among the living.
Then I turn my head,
listening to the fingers of a wind chime as they continue to clap.
As if applauding two little children
handing over that tiny piece of paper in the midst of a crowd.
The sound of hope echoes through their lungs.

Trumpet of the Herald

Turner Toliuszis

A cacophony of blended culture
reaches its mighty crescendo,
waves and wind hammering
mercilessly at vessels of frail hope.

The journey is difficult,
and the arrow misses its target.
Belief clings to a golden thread
of frayed harp string.
News comes in little belts
of whispers and music.
The herald's trumpet goes unheard
and the weak and strong go together.

Its orchestra reaches a high point,
crashing, crying, and desperately
clinging for survival, but serenity returns,
fortissimo becomes pianissimo.

The drum of many hearts ache for renewal.
A quest is ending as suddenly as it began.
Drums and trumpets whisper again.
There won't be an encore.

Why Choose to Risk It

Lily Barmoha

How dare you walk out of here,
with all your stuff and memories,
throwing it all in the back of your car,
and driving away.

The sight of you speeding away down the dirt road,
not looking back at your home,
is a sight I'll never see
if there's anything I can do about it.

Pathetically, I'll cling onto you,
like a child does to her mother.
Even if you throw all your determination and anger
into pushing me off, I'll never let you go.

You think I'm crazy, irrational!
This is all to protect you from the unknown dangers,
dangers you don't deserve to face,
they can't hurt you if you stay.

You always craved spontaneity,
that's just who you are,
but the line between impulsiveness and stupidity,
has vanished in your eyes.

High School Category – Aiken

Supernatural

Cameron Barron

Many a time we find ourselves in ignorance
Of the events around us
Not those of physical being
But those of supernatural
Often we are too afraid to open our eyes
to the possibilities of something else
Often we are paralyzed with fear
Often we dismiss the sounds and shadows
Often we try to explain the unexplainable
But never do we try to accept the truth
Never do we give in to the sinister feeling
Do not try to explain something that refuses to
make itself clear

Fragile

Jasmine Kitchings

A house has a window.
Some have two or three, while others have many more.
A window is made of glass with plenty to show.
Look through one and find the memories in store.
In one, a couple holding hands while walking along the sand.
Another, a newborn's cry fills hearts of the one's dear.
While a family moves into a new house on their land;
People go to a celebration, from far and near.
These memories will only hold for a short while.
A person gazing down at a loved one's grave.
Tears cover faces that can be seen for miles.
These memories forgotten, push away, and left unspoken.
The window remains cloudy as small cracks start to grow,
Till the window shatters, and remains there broken,
And he plants around the house spreading from the
pain it sows.
So, don't forget the memories you share.
Don't let your actions go nowhere.
Show your loved ones that you'll be there,
And that throughout life, you will always care.

Colors

Lizzy Kleinkauf

You took color samples of my words,
hanging them to dry
with your bad habits and bruised knuckles.
You painted me into your broken bottles,
smashing portraits into the wall.
You sewed me into your palms,
pulling the black and blue thread tight
around the hallows of my cheeks.
You caught me up in your flames
and I swallowed up your match-tip fingers
when they struck against me,
burning up my colors like wax.

Building Block

Brandi De Haven

As a building block I feel like I should warn you
The tallest towers tend to tumble hardest
Though being a standalone object is pointless
Unlike Your corners, let's be honest
People will come along and make you think you're someone
When in reality they just need another brick
They'll toss you aside when they're done, don't you see?
So don't believe them for a fraction of a clock's tick
You don't have to stand 'alone' to be in
dependent, though it may seem like the only way
You can build yourself up without stacking upon others,
Just give it some time, okay?

High School Category – International

If Forgiveness Was Made of Stardust

Sophia Giudici-Juarez

I am not an angry person.
I find that harboring resentment
like antique bomb shelters
only makes the Earth of my being heavier.

So I choose to eject grudges
until they are a speck of dust
in the horizon, blending in with stars
so that I do not know the difference
between my dreams and my nightmares.

I forget but never forgive,
call my monsters constellations
and give them names so as to
make them as fairytale-like as possible.

In a parallel universe, I am able
to live without these sinful angels,
but for now, I will bask in the glow
that these ghostly comets make.

If Forgiveness Was Made of Stardust

I choose to make a wish
instead of renouncing friendships
because even though I've never seen
a shooting star, I don't believe in
falsifying tragedy.

The Infinity of Possibility

Marina Ellis

There is no final sound of a song,
no finite numbers between zero and one,
and time knows no end.

A hymn holds an impossibly possible
number of fragments in a second,
the burdens between zero and one,
and so its melody knows no end.

The racing thoughts of an unspeakable reality
are still burning in the wrinkled folds of time,
hiding and stealing hope between zero and one,
and so my memories are as alive as I am
and trauma knows no end.

We are still on a spread of yellow-green bile
on tender white bedsheets,
he is still holding my thighs and pushing me closer
into the unmeasurable distance between zero and one,
and outside, the green forests remain
frozen in a universe that knows no end.

Her Voice

Jennifer Nguyen

Ah, did you hear did you hear did you hear then
The broken strains of notes from the high mountains?
Did you hear did you hear did you hear then
How the skies cry out in torment with wet tears,
Slabs of fat raindrops and broken lightning streaks,
Roars of the rolling clouds and choked-up thunder,
Hiccupping and coughing of heavy intervals,
Heaving the pain, lifting the pain, feeling the pain?
Did you hear did you hear did you hear then
The earth shakes with contorted spasms,
Twisted shapes of running shadow,
Etched on the stone-cold slab of our foundation?
Did you see, did you see, did you see then
How as nature is crying, it weeps for you too?

I think the bird sings in torment
Of its captive stage, of its held back wings,
Of its broken beak, of its darkened eyes
But I know why the caged bird sings
Because captive or not,
It will sing regardless of its capture,
It will sing because it believes in the free sky it flew under
Of the rivers and valleys it tumbled by
The song of the black birds of freedom and capture

Her Voice

Intermingle
Never think that the caged bird won't sing.
She spoke with a reverie to the air
Hand clutched tight the intangibility
Threads undone tangling around stumpy fingers
Wreaths stringing silk-thin petals perching on
thin hair strands
Slipping under inky threads, woven with the spring air.

Death of the Poèt

Nadia Dimtrova

The happy verses are his legacy.
The wondrous words of bliss he leaves are quenched.
The rumors are announced: contemptuously
the hostile crowd lynches the Poèt wretched.
Tell me, Poèt, unfortunate fellow,
who chained you to this miserable Earth?
The voices in my head, brother! – sorrow
sneaking, although his goal is to spread their mirth.
As he is trudging to his callous death
the whispers from inside him speak aloud.
Oh, Executioners, his final breath
salutes you as he loves you – mortal crowd.

The halo is stolen from his wise head;
But people put a wreath of thorns there instead.

Adult Mahogany Red Literary Prize

Racist Rice

Minncey Richani

I don't wash it excessively for W
araq Enab
Perhaps just once
Tipping out the excess diluted mi
lky pigmentation of water
Until the droplets are falling at an agitating pace
Every grain plumps up with heat you see
So the collection laying in my palm could be a handful
A couple of spoonfuls I've saved from
Sliding
through tubes along with morning fresh and mush
Just a quick glance at the sink
The aluminium highlighting numerous white rods
Helpless to do nothing but slip through the gaps between my fingers
And dance around above a wet layer
Just a quick glance
Lon
g enough to utter God forgives
Before blasting the tap and draining them
A short enough time to disallow any guilt to settle
And time and time again
Traditional dishes after the next
Wash, drain, waste

Racist Rice

Waraq Enab, Kousa Mehshi,
Or as a side with
Kafta and T
abouli
Feeding the drains
Instead of millions of hungry mouths
That have almost forgotten how rice tastes

Diamonds on the Rocks

Ellen Ricks

I am drunk again
On gin and glitter.
Tittering on black stilettos:
So this is how it goes.

"Keep Smiling" I tell the girl in the mirror.
I don't recognize her, I hope she's alright
Popping diet pills in feminist literature class,
Tap dancing on landmines.

They told me I could be anything,
So I tried to be a god.
You can be anyone's deity
If you know how to sparkle.

Once, I was pure. My body a temple.
I could refuse every need
Deluded by the belief that I want nothing.
Hunger told me I was divine.

Recovery tarnished my holy land
Men still prayed to me, coveted me.
I am disaster's child bride
No one else could claim me.

Diamonds on the Rocks

They continued their compulsion.
Luring sailors into my abyss,
Dragging them into the void.
Going down, sailors whispered "Siren."

They told me I was the best and brightest,
Till I washed up on the beach, glitter in my hair.
Now I'm a lighthouse, nightly and alone
Drinking diamonds on the rocks

The Death of a Poet

Kendall Driscoll

When sleep should come
and you perchance to dream,
I hope that life lost would be a tome
of ever

lasting stories and remembrances.
Between the lines
is the marrow of our existence
—
etched are the nights
we celebrated
until three
in the morning on a weekday
or those moments we laughed until our sides ached.
Being amongst life-
long friends
is the greatest happiness anyone can afford.
But what of the day
that we must leave the ones we love
and embark on a different road?
What
do we make of a poet's life
and death?

The Death of a Poet

Is
it
like a candle
—
a light of hope,
beauty,
and inspiration,
incandescently burning
with quiet passion
until the day
it is time
to fade
into the good night…

Paradise in Tears

Masoyo Has

No dark night passes into a new dawn without the sound of
a gunshot or a bomb blast or a heart shattering into a billion
pieces that even the beloved snow
Of the Himalayas fails to whiten the bloodied land.

Look, men from the plains and other homes have come
bearing banners of peace and order in your home.
But why do your women beat their breasts in distress?

Oh dearest sons! Bolt the doors closed.
Your women, more beautiful than ever,
let the mountain mists
clothe them in clouds for the winds are pregnant with terror.
Rivers and lakes lay frozen
as houses in flames light up the Valley sky
while the mountains echo your sisters' cries.

What has become of you, my son?
Have your dreams fled from your eyes?
Come take up your shining sword
lest this Paradise will turn into ashes.

Paradise in Tears

No soul shall mourn your death as you shine in your
beautiful brown Pheran,
Your tears settled in the riverbed of Jhelum,
The Chinars will have another story to store, of your death.

And of my brutal death, the Chinars bear witness
as they drown my battered body into the Wular.
And lo, the faithful leaves float with the wind to feel my soul
as I rise to the sky.

Impatience

Noel Pratt

The future has not been birthed and the present is not laid to rest. Why does tomorrow hide its splendor and today expose its flaws?
I was born two days too late only to die three days early.
What sick fate does this world espouse there is no partiality in finality.
In the depths of the soul lie seeds of greatness, why couldn't they already be trees?
Why do people run miles to condition their bodies, why doesn't a quick sprint meet the need?
Why does learning go on in an endless cycle?
Why couldn't we stop at just knowing right from wrong?
Why does success require, long term, repetitive commitment?
Why can't we all just win the lottery and be free?
Why is wisdom illusive and a thing to be sought? Why is foolishness abundant, lurking to run us down?

Senior Category

Red Ink on Miracles

Wendy MacLean

You cannot correct these mountains
like some child's arithmetic homework
they will never add up
the valleys alone
are exponentially beyond evaluation
the sum of humility and grandeur
can only be marked by prayer

I cry for relief
listening for the echo
to determine the distance
from my call
to your mercy
my voice returns to me
without judgement

only sunset has the authority
to use red ink
on these miracles

The Last Wildflower

Don Shook

Spring showers simply did not fall.
A hot south wind sustained.
And we were captured in the thrall
Of summer's brutal reign.

Our number, which had blossomed fair
In such a vast array,
Began to shrivel in despair,
Then died and fell away.

And that soft beauty we had brought
To this indurate land,
Remained but a decaying thought,
A mulch by Nature's hand.

Now I alone await the end
From which I will not cower;
Fragrant and bright, I will not bend.
I am the last wildflower.

Fear of Fire. Lower East Side, 1966

Terence Cady

The old woman does not sleep for fear of fire
in her fifth-floor walkup at the corner
of Second Avenue and Sixth Street.

Finally, around three a.m.
fatigue descends
and smothers her
until daylight stabs her back to life.

She turns on her companions,
the coffee maker first, and then
on shrunken limbs
she shuffles to the television.

She puts breadcrumbs on the pie plate
on the fire escape
to feed the birds, but
only pigeons come.

Once a day a nice lady
brings her meals, but
she is always "too busy" to sit
and talk awhile.

Fear of Fire. Lower East Side, 1966

Mrs. Gambi, the next-door neighbor,
just went clattering down the stairs,
on a rubber-covered gurney.
The siren was not on when the ambulance drove away.

The old woman is the only one left
on the fifth floor now, and
She does not sleep for fear of fire.

Ode to the Ravioli I Left Behind

Dianalee Velie

True to my fickle brain, I left you behind
in the Styrofoam to-go box, destined you
to the restaurant's trash bin instead
of providing me with two scrumptious lunches.

You were perfection, aglow in olive oil,
your little patty cakes of dough infused
with emerald spinach and filled with fluffy
ricotta. Sautéed peppers, broccoli
and mushrooms crowned your glory.

Oh, to leave such perfection behind.
Forgive me, please, and add this error
to the temple of my transgressions.

Unless of course, I pray, our server
took you home to relish after
her long shift, sitting in bed
with her boyfriend, seductively
feeding each other tiny morsels
of this stolen indulgence.

This would grant me
forgiveness and atonement.
This would clean my plate.

Winner Biographies

2016 Winners

Middle School Category

Mateo Strickland is an 8th grader who attends Miami Arts Charter. He majors in creative writing, and has been published to multiple competitions such as Young American Poets Digest and Creative Communication. He looks to add more publications to his growing list of achievements.

Isabella Matthei is a student at Miami Arts Charter in the creative writing department. She has never been published but wishes to be published some time. In her free time, she enjoys writing, reading, and watching political debates. In the future Isabella would like to work as a poet or screenwriter.

Alana Olivero is a writer who enjoys reading and writing in her spare time. She started writing when she was ten years old, and has since, followed her passion. She hopes that one day her work will be published to be enjoyed by readers of all ages.

Maia Tasker is a student at Miami Arts Charter School and she is enrolled in the Creative Writing Program. She likes to spend her free time writing, reading, and petting animals. She's interested in reading others' poetry, art, and listening to music.

Winner Biographies

High School Category

Daniela Antelo is a dedicated writer in 10th grade who is currently enrolled in the Creative Writing department in Miami Arts Charter School. She won a gold key for a collection of poems in the Scholastics competition as well as several silver keys in her short stories and nonfiction work. She has been published in the Orange Island Review, the Young Poets Anthology, Rattle etc.

Naomi Jeanpierre is adept at 3 languages: English, Bad English, and Gibberish. She has been published in several anthologies and aspires to be the author and an illustrator of her own book.

Nyaila Newbold is an 9th grade student at Miami Arts Charter School. She has been published by Young American Poetry Digest and won an honorable mention in the Scholastic Awards. She has three brothers, a dog she's in love with, and a phone she can't resist using.

Allyson Ifergan is a 15-year old living in Miami, Florida with her father. She loves music, red, walks in the evening, and spending time with the people she loves. She is fluent in French and English.

Adult Category

Gina Marie Mammano is a poet, non-fiction prose writer, spiritual director, and teacher residing on Whidbey Island in the state of Washington. Some of her deepest joys include hosting a local radio show, creating rites of passage, and using the salve of words to heal.

Amanda O'Mara graduated at Arkansas State University (B.S., journalism) and Seton Hall University (M.A., school counseling) in 2008. She recently moved from Virginia's eastern shore, where employed as a Career Coach for local college and high schools, to coastal North Carolina with her husband. O'Mara began writing poetry in 1993. She has lived in Arkansas, New York and South Carolina as well. Her love for nature, people, theories, philosophies and art are prevalent in her writing and photography. She may also be found experimenting with the culinary arts, participating in water sports and lots of movie watching!

David Morgan O'Connor is from a small village on Lake Huron. After many nomadic years, he is based in Albuquerque, where a short story collection progresses. He contributors monthly to: "The Review Review" and "New Pages". His writing has appeared in "Barcelona Metropolitan", "Collective Exiles", "Across the Margin", "Headland, Cecile's Writers", "The Great American Literary Magazine", "Bohemia", "Beechwood", "Fiction Magazine", "After the Pause", "The Great American Literary Magazine" (Pushcart nomination), "The New Quarterly" and "The Guardian". Tweeter: @dmoconnorwrites

Melanie Lucht is a twenty-three year old from Wisconsin. She has been writing poems and fiction since the age of eleven. In her spare time not spent writing, she enjoys reading a variety of genres and spending time with her nieces and nephews.

Winner Biographies

Senior Category

Nancy Louise Cook is a writer and teaching artist whose wanderlust has taken her to New England, New Mexico, the Atlantic Shore and, most recently, the frozen lakes of Minnesota. Her work has recently appeared in "Pacific Review", "Pilgrimage", "St Petersburg Review", and "Bengal Lights". She runs monthly free community writing workshops in Minneapolis and was last year's recipient of the "Lillian E. Smith Writer" in Service Award from Piedmont College.

Lee Patton enjoyed a free-range childhood on northern California's Mendocino Coast, attended college in Sacramento and the Bay Area, including Education School at San Francisco State and an MA in the University of Denver's Writing Program. He once developed an accidental career as a mystery novelist and woke from a ten-year spell as an accidental playwright to concentrate on fiction and poetry. In non-fiction, he's focused on political satire, travel, and environmental reportage.

Robert Ronnow's most recent poetry collections are *New & Selected Poems: 1975–2005* (Barnwood Press, 2007) and *Communicating the Bird* (Broken Publications, 2012). Visit his web site at *www.ronnowpoetry.com*.

Jeanie Greensfelder is the author of *Biting the Apple* (Penciled In, 2012), and *Marriage and Other Leaps of Faith* (Penciled In, 2015). Her poems have been published at "Writer's Almanac" and "American Life in Poetry", and the "On Being" blog;

WINNER BIOGRAPHIES

In anthologies: *Paris, Etc.*, *Pushing the Envelope: Epistolary Poems*, and *30 Years of Corner of the Mouth*; and in journals: "Askew", "Miramar", "Orbis", "Kaleidoscope", "Riptide", "Solo Novo", "Falling Star", "If&When", and others.

International Poet Category

Mima Kabwe: I enjoy writing poetry and short stories because I have loved to tell stories from a young age. I enjoy sharing my thoughts and feelings and I think that this contest is a great opportunity for me to showcase my work. I hold a BSc in Computer and Information Sciences from Monash University. I am from the DRC (Democratic Republic of Congo), but my family and I moved to South Africa when I was four years old. I enjoy writing poetry and short stories.

Graca N. Kibio: My name is Graça Kiboi and I am a 15-year-old girl from Nairobi, Kenya living in Seoul, South Korea. My hobbies include running track, reading history books, taking my dog on long walks and, of course, writing poetry.

Siya Ntsumpa has been published in "KOTAZ MAGAZINE", a small literary magazine in South Africa. He runs a small non-profit that works with disadvantage school children and rural schools.

Yvonne Wedgwood was born in Perth, now lives in Sydney. She worked as a Secretary in Australia, London, and Vancouver. She also was a Medical Secretary with U.S. Forces in Germany. On retirement did volunteer work with refugees and in the

Winner Biographies

Courts. She has a daughter and two granddaughters. Hobbies include reading, crosswords, gardening, cooking, beach, and football. She is interested in human rights, animal welfare, and travel.

2017 Winners

Middle School Dave Drake Award

Elyse Thomas is an 8th grade creative writer that attends Miami Arts Charter School. She has been published in several poetry anthologies and even performed on the stage of the Adrienne Arsht Center. She enjoys baking and reading books in her spare time while snuggling with her Maine Coon cat, Hazel, nicknamed-Hazy.

Angelina Minnittee: I am "a geek of a girl that loves to write". I was born in Miami and lived here all my life. My school is Miami Arts Charter, and I wouldn't have it any other way.

Turner Toliuszis is a responsible 7th grader who loves to read and is obsessed with felines. He enjoys writing and tries to stay on schedule when it comes to it.

Lily Barmoha has been going to Miami Arts charter for two years know. She studies writing with her teacher, Jen Karetnick, and that has helped her to grow as a writer in many ways. She won a Silver Key in Scholastics competition in 2017.

Winner Biographies

High School Category – Aiken

Cameron Barron: There isn't much to say about me other than I have done a lot in a little bit of time. I am a Girl Scout. I go to church. I am in the NJROTC. I am on multiple teams. The biggest thing about me, though, is that I love art. I love art more than anything. I lead a normal life. I have always been creative and curious. I always want to explore new places and try new things. I have a great family and wonderful life and honestly there isn't much else I would ask for.

Jasmine Kitchings: I love to read, write, draw, sing, and anything else that involves being creative. I enjoy writing poetry because it allows me to express my thoughts and feelings. I think literature is an important tool and can be used to make or start a change in the world.

Lizzy Kleinkauf: I have always enjoyed writing poems. I have spent a majority of my summers going to a gifted arts program for writing called GATEWAY. As much as I love writing poems, my plan, however, is to study Psychology and Law in college. My goal is to receive my doctoral degree in Psychology.

Brandi De Haven has been writing with intent for four years now, needless to say it's a passion that shows no sign of burning out. However, poetry isn't really her forte. But then again, neither is geometry, robotics, ukulele, or French, but she does those anyway. What a complete madman!

Winner Biographies

High School Category – International

Sophia Giudici-Juarez is a junior in Miami Arts Charter enrolled in the Creative Writing program. She has participated in the national spoken word competition "Brave New Voices". She was published in the Nation and has won several gold keys from Scholastics.

Marina Ellis is a junior at Miami Arts Charter. They have been published by "Canvas", "Open Minds Quarterly", "Poetry Matters", "Colorism Healing", "Literature Wales", and "World Enough Writers". Marina has been awarded two Silver Keys from Scholastic Art and Writing, first place in Florida's 2014 "Promising Young Writers essay" contest, and fifth place in the "Atlantic Institute's" 2014 essay contest.

Jennifer Nguyen is a student at Nossal High School, an academically selective entry school in Victoria, Australia. A lover of the English language and literature, she enjoys reading works that make her think and working on numerous (and often neglected) writing projects.

Nadia Dimitrova was born in the small town Pavlikeni, on 26 May 1998, but moved to Sofia – the capital of Bulgaria. Along with Nadia's love for sciences, she has cultivated a strong affection towards literature. Nadezhda is the Editor-in-Chief of the Lux literary magazine of AAS, as well as a published writer.

Winner Biographies

Adult Mahogany Red Literary Prize

Minncey Richani: A twenty-three-year-old Australian-Syrian Writer aspiring to not tell her story but to enthrall you, to have you experience your deepest fervors within her words, to tell your story.

Ellen Ricks has been published in "Revolving Doors Zine", "Oak Lit Magazine", "Potsdam People", and "North Country Literary Magazine". She was a finalist for the 2014 Norman Mailer Creative Writing award for 2-year colleges (creative nonfiction). She runs the fashion blog "Sarcasm in Heels".

Kendall Driscoll is the author of *Speech of the Masquerade*. Her work has been published in *Poetry Matters Anthology, Poetry Diversified, Poetry Diversified: A Human Experience Anthology*, and "The Echo" (Furman University's literary magazine). Driscoll earned a Bachelor of Music from Furman University and is currently pursuing a Master's degree in Music from Boston University.

Masoyo Has: Call me a person with a love for poetry that is immeasurable, I belong to a headhunting tribe called the Tangkhul Nagas. I write to promote peace and love and to bring the silenced voices alive through my poetry.

Noel Pratt: I am Noel Pratt. I am a husband, a father, a brother, and a son, who is seeking to relay his thoughts, imagination, and creativity through the medium of writing. I refuse to be restricted to a particular style or pattern. I trust you will enjoy reading as much as I enjoyed creating.

Senior Category

Wendy Jean MacLean is a poet and minister in a small country church in Eastern Ontario. In 2016 she won 1st and 2nd prize in the Drummond Literary Contest, and 1st prize in the Open Heart 11 Contest. Her work has also been put to music by Canadian composers. "The Stars Point the Way" won the Outstanding Composition Award and was published by Hal Leonard company. Her two books of poetry, *Rough Angel* and *Spirit Song in Ancient Boughs*, were published by Borealis Press.

Don Shook is a past president of the Fort Worth Poetry Society is a writer, actor, director, and producer who has worked with such stars as Dick Clark, Cybill Shepherd, Debbie Reynolds, and Betty Buckley. Formerly with NBC in New York, he has performed in theatre, film, and television across the country including Carnegie Hall, New York City and five years as a resident performer at Casa Manana Musicals in Fort Worth. He was named by "Angels Without Wings" as the 2009 Senior Poet Laureate of Texas for his poem "This Too Shall Pass" and has written five novels and an acting handbook Entitled *Actors Soup*, self-published in 2014.

Terence Cady is a trial lawyer and nationally certified child welfare law specialist, who graduated University of California, Berkeley in 1965. He is 74-years old. Credits include, *My Friend the Zodiac Killer* (non-fiction), *The Storyteller* (Sept. 09), and

WINNER BIOGRAPHIES

Honorable Mention in New Millenium New Writers Contest for a revised version of *My Friend the Zodiac Killer*, "Searching For The Graves of My Ancestors; The Kerr's Creek Massacres" (Lexington, Virginia area, 1700s), published in 2014 by The Mountain Laurel.

Dianalee Velie is the Poet Laureate of Newbury New Hampshire where she lives and writes. She is a graduate of Sarah Lawrence College, and has a Master of Arts in Writing from Manhattanville College, where she has served as faculty advisor of Inkwell: A Literary Magazine. She has taught poetry, memoir, and short story at universities and colleges in New York, Connecticut, and New Hampshire and in private workshops throughout the United States, Canada, and Europe.